SUNSHINE -The Joy of Soul Poetry Volume 1

Usha Shree V

BookLeaf Publishing

India | USA | UK

Presentation by *BookLeaf Publishing*

Web: www.bookleafpub.com

E-mail: info@bookleafpub.com

ISBN: 9789360947897

First edition 2024

DEDICATION

To my loved ones and "SUNSHINE",

This book is dedicated to all of my family members, cousins and dearest friends who have inspired, encouraged and supported me throughout my journey.

To my father, M. Vasanth Kumar, who truly believed in the magic of my words and my abilities as a writer.

To my mother, Geetha Sudha V, who has been an unwavering pillar of strength, always there to lift me up.

To my husband, Vikash Kumar and my beloved daughters, Aaradhya Rajput and Aaditi Rajput, my nephew Rian Naidu, the lights of my life who fill every day with wonder and joy.

To my dearest brother, Pramod, whose love and encouragement furled my passion and my sister-in-law, Anamika, who has always been my strength and support.

To my late grandmother, Shyamala Devi, my first mentor and guide who ignited my passion for writing. who hails from the esteemed family of Sarojini Naidu (the Nightingale of India).

Lastly Priyanka C, my sunshine whose friendship has always brightened my path immeasurably.

Special thanks to all my dearest friends, cousins and my well wishers without whom, this book would have not been completed.

Words seem inadequate to express my gratitude to each of you for nurturing my talents and bringing out the best in me. This book is a testament to your boundless belief and profound impact on my creative journey.

ACKNOWLEDGEMENT

First and foremost, I want to express my profound gratitude to the Universe for the boundless love, blessings and guidance that have illuminated my path towards self-discovery and authenticity. This journey has been one of profound growth and transformation, and I am forever thankful for the abundance that has flowed into my life, allowing me to embrace my true, authentic self.

Thanking the universe for conspiring in my favour, by showering me with opportunities to learn, grow and evolve.

I am grateful for the challenges that have tested my resilience, for they have taught me invaluable lessons about perseverance, courage and the power of faith.

To my family, friends, and loved ones, thank you for your unwavering belief in me, even when I doubted myself. Your love and encouragement have been the wind beneath my wings, lifting me up whenever I faltered and reminding me of my worth and purpose.

I am eternally grateful for the unseen forces that guided me, gave me strength during the hardest moments and cleared the path for this work to emerge into the world. To my soul family, spiritual guides, ancestors and all who held the vision for my highest self - THANK YOU!

This book is a manifestation of the divine guidance that has graced my life and I am eternally thankful for the abundance that has made this journey possible. May these pages inspire others to embrace their authentic selves, to trust in the Universe's plan and to live a life of joy, fulfilment and boundless love.

PREFACE

This soulful book of poems is intended to guide readers on a spiritual journey of self-discovery and awakening to their true authentic nature.

"Within these pages, a symphony of soulful poems awaits - arising from the depths of human experiences, emotions and an eternal longing to understand life's profound questions. Why me? Why this phase? For those seeking illumination, these verses aim to unveil your ultimate purpose."

The insights collected here have emerged from the depths of my Soul through intense self-reflection, spiritual seeking and the truths I needed to embrace.

At our core, we are all spiritual seekers yearning to arise the phoenix within. This collection is a labor of love, intended to awaken you to the magic inherent in nature and this human journey. May the words vibe a resonance that stirs your soul and helps uncover your most authentic self.

This offering is a humble attempt to reach past the mind and into the heart-space of millions.

The purpose is to help each individual find their inner sunshine - that brilliant light which shows the way home to your true essential nature and ignite to become their true "Authentic self".

To Find Her in My Solace

Amidst the lush of green valley,
Pearls of water flowing,
Embracing the vast everlasting blue sky,
Sits a brown-eyed lass!

Green, blue, silvery, white,
Blissful was every moment.
Overwhelmed with joy,
Lost in her Solitude.

The dance of the fluttering leaves,
The cool breeze humming the hymn,
Sparkling was her mesmerising eyes,
Unveiling thousands of emotions!

Smiling amidst the misty greens,
While I approached to catch a glimpse,

Saw her vanishing in the cloudy dust,
Never to return from the hovering clouds.

Strolling in the dark night,
Solace accompanied by the star-studded sky,
While I happened to acquaint her,
Only to find her lost amidst the mist!

Saw her dancing in the showers of rains,
While I stepped in, to lead the moves,
Like a thunderbolt she vanished,
Wide awakened like that from a mystical dream.

Cuddling the lovely white puppies,
Saw her playing and huddling,
Just when I happened to embrace one,
Saw her explicitly disappear in the horizons.

Gazing still at the endearing rainbow,
Celebrating a thousand colours of joy,
While lost at this memorising sight,
Like an angel, she fluttered away in the dusky
shine of light.

Little did I know, "To find her in my solace"!
The mystical magic of nature.
Uncovering thousands of secrets untold,
The answers to all the life's puzzles!

In the journey of life,
If ever you find bliss in solace,
It is only then you realise,
Solitude Hymn a journey of eternal bliss!

The Surreal Voyage of the Botanist

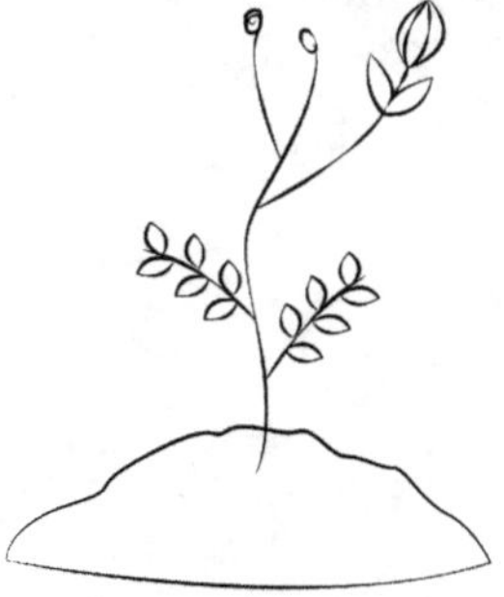

The timeless epic of 18th century,
The dreams of an unwavering girl from France.

So adventurous and dangerous,
A life full of disguise.

Weaving dreams to travel the world,
When women weren't allowed.

A journey of a brave botanist,
An adventurous vivid destination to reach.

When the dreams were so magical,
Who could dare to picture the surreal reality?

The audacity in her,
To dream of her passion.

The journey to be travelled,
To an unknown destination, again to another.

So talented and ambitious,
Her intentions so strong.

When the world gave reasons to lose,
She stood determined amidst all odds.

Nothing could replace,
Her aspirations that high.

Accompanying the royal botanist, Philibert
Commerson,
A young valet climbing icy mountains.

Hunting exotic animals,
Carrying two pistols, not someone to mess with.

Disguised as a man,
She set for a surreal voyage.

To travel the world with a passion of gathering
plants,
The only ambition of the botanist.

She sailed the entire globe,
Exploring the life of her dreams.

With all her free will,
Facing challenges, obstacles many.

Never to lose hope,
Only to return triumphantly.

Passion filled her heart,
So pure and intense.

Was she a warrior princess or-
A destined ambitious voyager?

She became the first woman to sail around the
globe,
"Jeanne Baret", was her name though.

I rather call her, 'Danger in seas',
or "The heroine of the 18th century".

A remarkable story to unfold,
An epic of adventure, disguise and danger.

Lost in the history and place, she was one of a
kind,
To ignite the passion in many, to inspire
thousands.

Live your passions, a message to all,
Embark on your journey of self-discovery.

Strong People Do Cry

Who said-
Strong people don't cry.

Cry, if you want to,
Laugh out if you have to.

No limits, no boundaries,
For being yourself!

Emotions are to be felt,
Anger, guilt, shame or joy!

It's okay to cry,
It's okay to wipe them dry.

It's okay to express anger,
It's okay to shout out for help.

Nothing to suppress,
Nothing to pretend!

No fear of judgement,
Neither anyone to belittle!

Slow down if required,
Or pause if you really want to.

Life is not a race,
It's a journey of feelings and experiences.

We are made of emotions,
Who said it's wrong to express?

Strong people do cry and then rise,
A new day awaits, to shine, to conquer!

The Mysteries of Life

Birth and death,
Eternal dance of life,
Some lose and some win,
The mystery of life unknown!

Not every battle,
Is to be fought,
You can also dance in peace,
And win the war losing battle!

A night completes a day,
The cycle of new hopes of joy,
Every night rests,
With a new light of tomorrow!

Pain exists in happiness,
Life is nothing without it.
Happiness cannot be embraced,
Unless pain is ever tasted!

In the symphonic dance of life,
Every single victory,
Witnesses the pride,
By defeating the fear within!

Love lies in hate,
Hate dies in love.
Impossible to hate without loving,
And love is difficult where hate hails!

Live a life of dignity,
Never to die.
Dying for a life of serenity,
Is where the beauty lies!

Friend turns to foe,
When enmity is disclosed,
Being a friend of a foe,
Has never been justified for either!

In every attachment,
You will always detach.
Only after you get attached,
The pain of detachment is felt!

The vibrancy of Yin and Yang,
Energies of the moon and the earth,
When life is full of blacks,
A soulful pinch of white awaits!

The mysteries of life,
No one has ever known.
The beauty in the ugliness,
And the ugliness hidden beneath the beauty!
None are good,
Neither are bad,
All dance selflessly,
To the mysterious rhythm of life!

Clinging to the Cliff

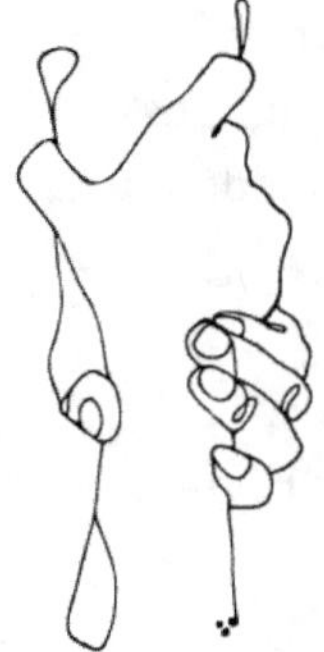

I see you clinging,
Holding on to the edge.

Fearless and stuck,
Confused and cluttered.

The sight of the valley,
The rocks and the greenery down.

Clinging to the cliff,
Most exciting experience one could have!

Life is paused, every moment precious,
All we need, a hand to lift.

The power of clinging in between,
Two choices of life and death.

One step upwards,
Life to explore.

One slip downwards,
An eternal world welcomes.

One move can change everything,
One step is all it needs.

In the story of our life,
We are often seen clinging to the cliff.

Clinging between decisions,
Choices or paths to be taken.

The confusion or the dilemma,
Often tending to bring chaos.

Nothing is right, none is wrong,
Stuck in between, is worst of all.

Life is, when that one decision is made,
Right or wrong, who cares?

The power in choosing,
Is the ultimate power of self.

A life to live, a heart to love,
The audacity to accept what our soul seeks.

The will of winning,
Surpasses all the fear within.

That one ultimate step is all that matters,
At the end, "Authentic you" always wins!

The Power of Time

Time unfolds the mysteries of life,
Unveiling the colours of everyone.

The role of time is so mystical,
Right things happen, at the right time!

Time plays its role so precisely,
Revealing the untold secrets timely.

Time seems so surreal,
When in the arms of the beloved.

Time is the only witness,
To the swirling moments of good or bad.

Time is just a reflection,
To showcase the beauty of self.

The power of timing is only felt when,
Right things happen at absolutely wrong times.

Time is irreversible,
Once gone, gone forever!

Live in the moment,
Live to the fullest.

Time can never be seized,
Nor can be relived.

Time is only once,
After which, we only can regret.

Time is never partial,
Be it rich, miser or poor!

Time is the medicine to many,
Everything seems to heal over time.

Time is a saga of melody,
To all in agony.

Time is a weapon to fight all odds,
Wait for the time to be yours!

Time is precious, so is life,
Believe in the right timing of life!

Time is the only reminder,
To live our life to the fullest.

Lost Self

Is your eyes, in search of self?
Instead of wailing outside,
It's time to look within,
Beyond your inner self.

Look for the serenity in you,
Instead of being ruckus,
Embrace your fears and insecurities,
With grace accept oneself!

This is "YOU",
Your authentic self,
Amidst all times and odds,
You have ignored your authenticity.

Where is your humanity?
Your might and your sword.
The love for self,
And for others.

The purpose is lost,
So are you.
Never too late,
For the search to begin.

A journey within self,
To embrace, to heal.
Conquering the fears,
Lost self to find.

The one, once ruled,
With pride so high.
It's time to fight,
The odds within.

You are the grace,
You are the triumph,
You are the lost self,
Serenade your soul with harmony!

One day you will find,
Your lost self, your might.
The identity of your self,
The power of the authentic you.

Take a Pause

Whenever, you are stuck,
Feeling exhausted,
Quite confused,
Take a pause.

Whenever, amidst chaos,
Feeling suffocated,
Pain is all you feel,
Take a step back.

Whenever you are energised,
Feeling channelised,
Find your peace,
Find your solace.

Life is not perfect,
Everyone has their pace,
It's okay to slow down,
To take, one step at a time.

You can take some light,
A little hope,
Some belief of mine,
Until you find yours!

Symphony of Extremities

The darkness in the light of life,
The ray of light in the darkened path.

The tears of joy,
On the sun-kissed cheeks.

The long-lost laughter,
In search of tears of joy.

Emotions swirling,
In the depth of life!

The dance of Yin and Yang,
Eternal bliss unfolded.

Sunrise is a gift reborn,
Bliss of a new today.

In every sunset lies a hope,
Promises a beautiful tomorrow.

In the profound truth of love,
Lies a hidden gem of hatred.

In the game of life and death,
The symphony of extremities lies!

Memories

Lingering memories,
Moments once lived,
Fading twilights,
Roads once traveled.

Every moment to be relived,
This time, a fresh perspective,
The colours of dreams seen,
In the rainbow of moments lived.

The song once sung,
Only to intensify,
The glory of love,
In every lyrical beauty of life!

The lost souls once again,
Meet in the realms of love.
It's just not the same,
The bond stronger than ever!

Mystical Magic of Words

Words can make,
Words can break,
Words can be mesmerising,
Words can be traumatising.

The power of words,
Unseen or untold,
The mystical magic of words,
Has the power to change.

Words are vibrations,
Words are magical,
Words can unite,
Words can destroy.

The intentions of words,
Have the power to manifest,
Words are healing,
In the journey of life.

Embrace the Change

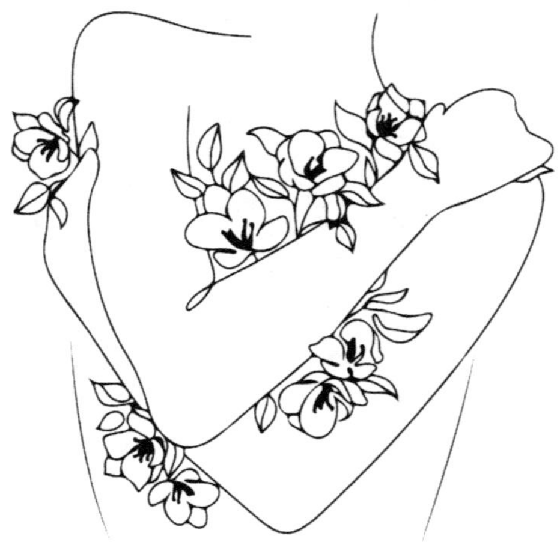

Change is inevitable,
Change gives power.

It's a mystical journey,
From innocence to maturity.

Change happens to all,
Be it kids to the old.

We witness the changes in many,
The seasons to the nature.

The change of emotions,
So are the feelings.

Change is the only alpha,
For the theta and gamma.

None would escape change,
Nor did yang or yin.

Embrace the change in you,
With all might and grace.

The Clouds

The silvery white clouds,
Wandering in the blue sky.

Flying free as a bird,
Floating high, puffy fluffy clouds.

I see you dance,
To the symphony of rains.

When the lightning strikes,
You sparkle like a twinkling star.

There is always a bright spot,
In the dark hovering clouds.

I wish to cuddle and embrace you,
In the dreamy world of fantasy.

Hey clouds, hold me tight,
And let's flee and tour the world above.

Dancing the night away,
Witnessing the symphony of showers.

Hey silvery, white clouds,
Are you an angel or a fairy in disguise?

You bring the bright sunshine,
A silvery shine in the world of blues!

Whimsical Stars

Twinkling, Dazzling,
All along the enchanting realm,
Captivating like whimsical artwork,
Glittering stars sprinkled,
Around the vast blue sky,
Paradise of sparkling lights!

The one shining bright,
Right beside the mesmerising moon,
Bestowing solstice blessings,
Mystical experience of night,
The pole star, guiding star,
Casting magical spells on many.

The shooting star, wishing star,
Has been mesmerising all,
The one who sees, is the one who wishes,

The surreal dreams turning into reality,
Twinkling, gleaming,
The shimmery pathway to the realm!

Twinkling, glimmering,
Endless is your count of blessings,
Ethereal and surreal,
The red stars, the cold stars,
Found in the galaxy of stars,
The whimsical art of stars!

The Joy of Sunshine

Sunshine, Sun bright,
Dancing elegantly in grace,
With all your mighty aura,
Wondering how you dazzle,
In the array of light,
Beauty of light that truly beckons!

Sunshine, Sun bright,
Like a Goddess Divine,
Walking alone in the aisle,
With so much of radiance,
I gazed in awe as your rise,
Your shine so ethereal!

Sunshine, Sun bright,
Hey magnificent you,
The mesmerising view,
Nothing can overpower you,
With so much light you shine,
Much more brighter and joyful forever!

Sunshine, Sun bright,
Your powers of light,
Endearing the dance of life,
The journey to the horizon sky,
An embarking expedition to explore,
Embracing the joy of sunshine!

Colours of Life

In the rainbow of life,
I have seen blues in the gloomy you.

Yellows in the sunshine kissing cheeks,
The calming greens amidst the uncertain woods.

Felt your whites in the purity of your soul,
Irreplaceable are the pinks of your innocence.

Seen you fight the blacks of your battles,
Lovely are the scars of grey.

How can someone shine orange bright?
While filled with the agonies of crimson red.

I see you shielded by a golden Aura,
While you are lost in your purples of life.

In a world filled with browns,
You are the silver in the rainbow of my life.

Set Yourself Free

Lost in the ocean of thoughts,
Overwhelmed by the torment of emotions.

Every thought of yours,
Every emotion you feel is just a belief.

The beliefs you created are an excuse,
It's the fear within.

Find the courage,
And Set yourself FREE.

Everyone has a story,
Every moment is a belief you create.

Beliefs are Thoughts,
Beliefs are Feelings.

Realign your thoughts,
Realign your belief system,

The more you break your pattern,
The more your situation improvises.

Find yourself aligned,
And Set yourself FREE.

Cosmic Journey

A story untold,
Dream unseen,
A journey untraveled,
Path untaken!

Then why-
Are these instincts,
So Strong-
And So intense!

A hidden message,
An unveiled truth,
Unfolding a vivid-
Mystic destination!

Long awaited,
Magical way,
Uncovering life,
A new dimension!

A journey unknown,
To the cosmic,
And beyond light,
Of compassion and care!

Is this a DREAM-
Or a reality unknown?
To live a life,
Moment to moment!

A story untold,
Dream unseen,
A journey untraveled,
But the Destiny destined!

Letter for Self

It's hard to believe,
The love I hold for you,
This is the time,
To look into the eyes in the mirror!

Feel your worth,
Tell time and align yourself,
For an experience here,
Letting the feeling pass by you!

Allow the agony to feel you,
A New hope, new love,
New beginning, new era of Self,
Begins a new phase of self-discovery!

You suddenly feel the calmness,
In the torment of emotions.
Wandering heart finds solace,
In the midst of NATURE!

The love for yourself,
Is so selfless and worthy,
Begins to speak the language of the universe,
To self and others!

Divine You

Emerge like the phoenix,
Dazzle like a diamond.

Casting an ethereal and radiant light,
Conquering all the fears and pain.

Smile at your broken self,
Align everything that seems so scattered.

Awaken the Goddess within,
Hey DIVINE YOU - of peripheral vision.

Feel the cocoon of love for yourself,
Emerge and blossom as a butterfly!

You are so uniquely beautiful,
Which no soul can ever replace!

Hey Princess! Hold your head high,
For you never doubt your self-worth!

You are the one, the world is waiting-
The divine driven You - AWAKE!

For only after the darkest night,
Will emerge the "DIVINE YOU -THE
SUNSHINE"

A Silent Whisper

The language of heart-
A Silent Whisper!

To all those who fear,
Fear is loud, intuition is calm.

So is peace-
The home of heart!

The calm you find,
In the hearts of love.

Is the start of your journey-
Of mystical wonders!

The language of heart-
A silent whisper!

Thousands of words spoken,
All in vain.

For a silent whisper-
Screams aloud!

Just a glance,
Gateway to your soul.

A gesture of comfort,
And intuition ignites.

The language of heart-
A silent whisper!

Trust your gut,
Listen to the energies.

Vibrations are magical,
That bridges your souls.

Shaken by the silence,
No wonder emotions speak.

The one who reads,
Your instincts in silence.

Knows the language of your heart-
A silent whisper!

Healing is a Journey

I see you heal,
With so much care,
Patience and kindness,
Compassionate to self.

Healing is universal,
It's an everyday ritual,
Happy or sad,
Overwhelmed or underwhelmed.

Healing is soothing,
Believe in the process,
Brings out the audacity,
To accept the authentic you!

Your kind words, your deeds of goodness,
Your actions of generosity,
Your kindness in helping others,
For all you have is your true self!

A winding soulful journey of self,
Be it physical or emotional,
In nature or in spirits, embracing your new self,
Heal yourself, for now and ever,

The pain in you is what meant to be,
Nobody is yours, nothing is yours!
Neither your body or mind,
Nor your wealth or possessions.

Heal and help others heal,
From the scars of the past trauma,
Heal from the words, from the insecurities,
Heal by the gratitude for the bitter experience.

Healing needs time,
Uncovering the layers of self,
The hidden wounds unseen,
Accepting self with grace!

Symphony of Nature

Dancing amidst the rainbows,
Playing with the dew drops,
I see myself crossing,
The bridge of rainbow to sunshine!

Singing amidst the orchestra of dark night,
A symphony of star-studded night,
I see myself dazzle,
In the ramble to moonlight!

Embracing the blue everlasting sky,
Never to let it go,
I see myself engrossed,
In the heartwarming heights of blue!

Pearls of Tears

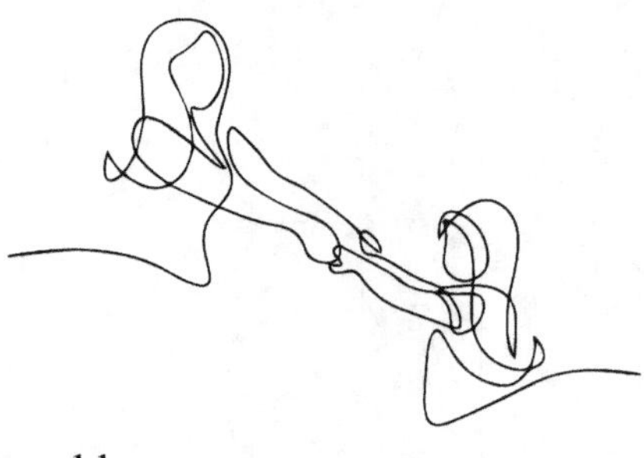

So vulnerable,
So effortlessly you flow,
So hard-hearted,
Your ego seems no more!

Whenever I see you,
With so much of grace,
Am left so dumbstruck,
So selfless, So you!

So insensitive,
So ignorant..
There is none who care,
To see you smile is very rare!

Your value so invaluable,
You deserve better,
Ignite your lost self,
Hey, precious pearl!

You are the dream come true,
In the world of joy,
Not everyone deserves you,
Hey pearls of TEARS!

The Rope of Hope - Rebirth

The love I lost,
The life I lived,
Nothing was true,
Until I met you!

The rope of hope,
The love for life,
Was only once,
When I truly lived!

First time I held you,
Was the love,
I always craved,
My baby, my love!

The first touch,
Your lingering smell,
What more can I ask?
Purest love ever bestowed!

Your cute round face,
The twinkling eyes,
Tiny toes,
The love unfolded!

The life I lived,
Was never the same,
The profound reason of rebirth,
For every baby, a mother is reborn!

The Enchanted You

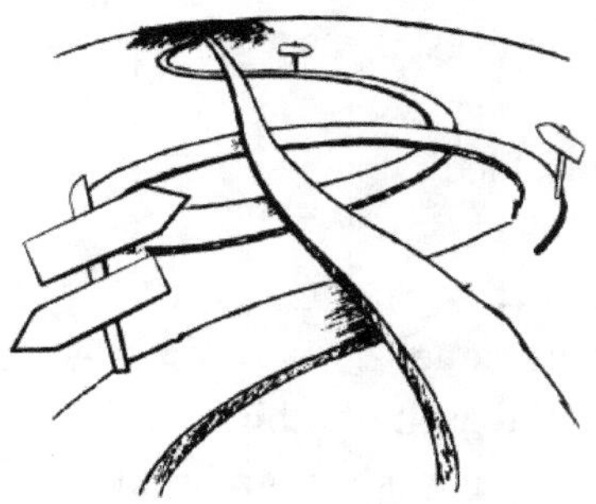

An epic of untold wonders,
Captivating the truth within,
Embarking the inevitable,
A journey to be travelled.

A Surreal journey?
Or a mesmerising expedition.
A reality to explore,
Embarking a vivid beauty!

An ethereal illustration,
Or a captivating journey,
To a vivid destination
Of mystical reality!

The enchanted,
A world of richness,
Discovery of self,
A reality to light!

Nature's Bliss

When you embrace the colours of rainbow,
The journey of life blossoms!

You begin to see the whites in the blacks.
The best in the worst!

The rising sun gives a new hope,
To rise and again rise!

It's only after the phases we undergo,
The beauty of full moon is seen, an authentic
self.

A garden of colourful flowers,
Reminds us of the beauty of emotions!

The calmness of the flowing rivers,
Directs you to always go with the flow!

In the vast everlasting blue sky,
You will find your limitless opportunities.

The star-studded beautiful night emphasises,
To identify the unique self as the brightest Star!

In the journey of life,
Each of us is here for a "Unique Experience"!

Allow yourself to engross consciously,
To live every moment with a purpose of joy!

Self Love

It's okay not to be "Okay",
It's okay to say a "NO",
It's okay to set your "Boundaries",
It all begins with "Self Love"!!!

It's okay to express your "Emotions",
It's okay to step "Aback",
It's perfect to fall in love with "Oneself",
It all connects with "Self Love"!!!

It's okay to be just "Yourself",
It's okay to "Prioritise" you over others,
It's okay to be "Kind" to ourself,
Living authentic is "Self Love"!!!

Elements of Life

The vast everlasting blue sky,
    The most powerful,
Cool healing waters,
    The evergreen healing nature,
The earth beholds,
    The fiercest dance of vibrancy,
Reminds the fire within,
    The rage to succeed,
Amidst all odds of life
    Is the Beauty it bestows!

The cool breeze, the blowing winds,
    The storms or the raging tempest.
Amidst the ranging dance of air,
    It is graceful in every gesture,
The sky, the water, the earth,

The fire and the air,
So soulful are the elements of life.
The energies, so vibrant,
Adding colours of joy,
In every aspect of LIFE!

Motherly Nature

The everlasting range of greens,
 Is all I see in every wilds.

However subtle you are,
Yet so powerful.

However playful you are,
Yet so mindful.

However selfless you are,
Yet so blissful.

The grace you carry,
Rejuvenating is your presence.

The love you bestow,
Heals anyone instance.

Hey motherly "Nature",
Is green your colour, blues or whites?

While I wander in your greens,
The soulfulness is all I feel.

Nothing more, nothing less,
Nature's blessings is all I seek!

Smile

Smile a mile,
While you smile.

Smile in your pains,
Smile in the rains.

The smile of triumph,
Seen in your trumps.

Smile every moment,
Nevertheless, even in torment.

Smile is rare,
Authenticity is fair!

Smile in grace,
In every life's pace.

Smile in gratitude,
Smile with all your attitude.

Smile is contagious,
Even when you are outrageous.

Smile like a baby,
Smile while others are nosy.

Smile in silence,
While you notice malice.

Smile in your power,
Creating the vibe forever!

Smile a while,
While you smile!

Rages and Serenity

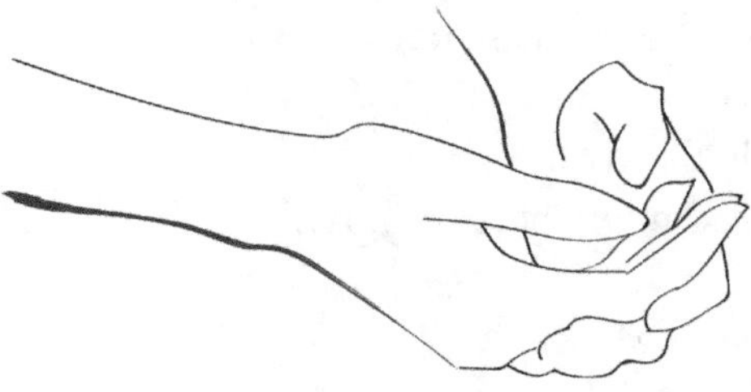

All the while,
What I thought was right,
Was never the same,
Until I acquainted my inner self!

The long lost myself,
Is when I found,
The balance between,
Rages and Serenity!

The calmness I found,
Within my inner self,
While fighting the anguish of-
World and life!

The long lost path I found,
Between the rages and tranquil,
Serenity is where I found,
The eternal bliss, authentic self!

The Story of Life

Life unfolding the pages,
All the bests and all the odds.

Be it good, be it bad,
All had a reason to showcase!

Accepting every challenge,
Time had put to test.

Belittled to our understanding,
Whatever we undergo and understand.

Karma is the ultimate balance,
Of our acts and rewards.

It's just the magic of timing,
Do we know what we owe?

The phases of life begin,
Good over evil, tranquil over chaos.

The time had to play its part,
Unfolding the laws of life.

Journey of life, an untold mystery,
Amidst all odds, destiny finally arrives!

The showers of peace, the voice of triumph,
All seems aligned, the story of life!

Hold on to Love

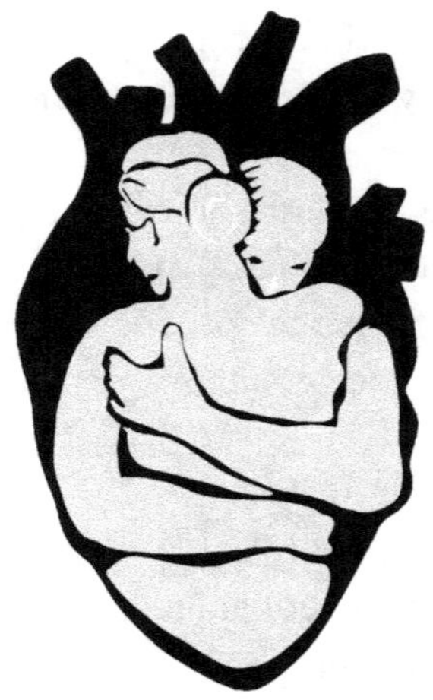

Hold on to your love,
Be it months or years,
You were the only one,
She had ever dreamt of.

You were her love,
Her breath and her pride,
Only hero she could look upon,
Her love so intense and serene.

No one ever knew the depths,
Of what she ever felt,
Lost are all those moments,
Buried deep beneath the sea.

It's now the time again,
To rise like a whirlpool,
Rewinding the wheel of time,
Reliving every single moment spent.

Relieving the past gruesome days,
Only to find the lost pearl of love,
Sunken deep inside the ocean,
The love that none could ever replace.

Hold on to your love,
For you were the only one,
Whom the heart ever belonged,
Not just for days or months, but eternity!

Soulful Sounds of Nature

The song of the roaring waves,
The music of the cool breeze,
Mesmerising sounds of nature,
Is a therapy by itself!

The rustling of the leaves,
The calmness in the flowing rivers,
The symphony of music,
So soulful, So peaceful!

The rhythms of the chirping birds,
The fluttering butterflies,
The serenity of Mother Nature,
Precious gift to mankind!

The humming of insects,
The squeaking of squirrels,
Immerse yourself in the soulful sounds,
With nature's harmony!

The soothing whispers of the wild winds,
The musical rhythm of the rains,
Embrace your soul,
Blissful escape to nature's symphony!

You are the Sunshine

I love to see the sunshine,
In the gloomy you,
Rise and shine with radiance,
Amidst the prevailing darkness.

It's only a matter of time,
All will pass by the sunshine,
The moments will be memories soon,
Embrace the you and shine!

You are the sunshine for all,
Your shine will brighten many,
All I wonder, how ignorant you are.
Could sun ever lose its radiance!

You are the sunshine bright,
No matter if the sun ever sets,
This is just a phase to pass,
A new ray of hope awaits to shine!

Look within for the light,
Bring out the power you endear,
Hey sunshine! You pave the path to many,
Embrace your self-worth and realign!

Eternal Love

The love for you,
Is so surreal and strong.

Nothing is irreplaceable
Nothing is more powerful.

The beauty of time,
Surpasses the beauty of love.

The love my heart holds,
Is beyond the earth and the skies.

The dream once dreamt,
The world once lived.

The love for you,
Is more than just an emotion.

The lingering memories,
The moments of joy reminds.

The love once lived,
The journey once planned.

The life of eternal love,
Was just an illusion of nothingness.

Seasons of Joy

The joy of flowering I see,
In the blooming buds.

The captivating landscape,
Of the lush green valleys.

The first rays of the dawn,
In the midst of the stormy night.

The only joy of pouring rains,
From the dark hovering clouds.

Joy of cherishing memories,
From the moments of past.

The joy I always embraced,
Watching the sunset into the yellowish sky.

The Joy I see in your twinkling eyes,
Eternal bliss of Seasons of joy!

The Bliss Within

The bliss you see,
In the life you live,
Every breath you take,
Is a blessing,
Reminding us,
Of being alive!

When you start,
To see the bliss,
In the smallest of things,
Count your blessings,
Endless are your gifts,
The eternal love of thee!

We are lost in the game,
Accumulating and losing,
The materialistic things,
Little do we know,
The sole purpose of living,
The joy in giving!

Lost in search of wealth,
Thriving endlessly over time,
It's now to deep dive,
The humility, the kindness,
The honesty and our purity,
The real quest within!

Mystery of the Wandering Mind

Lost in the past,
Worrying about future,
Disconnected ideas,
Flashes of random memories,
Begins the mystical journey,
Of the wandering mind!

A journey unbound
Neither to time, Nor to place,
Travelling from one thought to another,
One place to another,
One moment in past,
The next in future.

Scattered plans,
Wandering thoughts,
Living the fantasies unseen,

Being aware of the present,
Processing every single emotion,
Thoughts back to the moment!

Embrace the journey,
The process seems natural,
Sparks your creativity,
Finding solutions to many,
Unattended problems paves way,
A boon to the wandering mind!

Stillness

Lost in the woods of self,
Stillness I long,
In the wandering you,
In the broken you!

Authenticity is all I prefer,
In your eyes,
In your words,
In every aspect of you!

The calmness,
The mindfulness,
Thoughts realigned,
Joy in solace is all I find.

In the stillness of you,
Simplicity adheres,
The gratitude-filled self,
An ultimate gift for soul.

The Colours of the Dawn

The saga of dance,
Between the blacks and the whites.

Light and the darkness,
Everyday awaits a new colour of joy.

Brighter than the rainbow,
Are the colours of the dawn.

The first rays of yellowish sun,
Are a feast for the eyes.

Oh! The vast blue sky,
How you turned to crimson yellow.

Looks, as thousands of yellowish arrows,
Penetrating the sky.

Bright shiny rays of light,
Captivating millions of souls.

Bridging the body and soul,
Life to eternal bliss!

The colours of the dawn,
Brings endearing joy to all!

Peace over Love

All begins with love,
Heartfelt words, lovely gestures,
Mesmerising ways,
Endearing profound love.

Like that of a princess,
My every thought was heard,
Nowhere to be found now,
The traces of royalty.

The journey of love,
Has faded over time,
Or it's just me overwhelming,
Alas! Only the pain prevails.

The dream which I once cherished,
Suddenly turning to reality,
Only to realise its worth,
Just an illusion of thoughts.

At the end love wins,
Is what the world says?
A soulful choice to make,
"PEACE" over love - is what I say!

Endless Dreams

Lost in a mystical land,
I happened to see the flashes.
The first thing ever noticed was,
The blooming red buds.
The evergreen carpeted leaves.
Living in an experience,
No logic, no purpose,
No connection, no time bound.

Anything is bound to happen,
Anywhere I could be found,
Flying high in the heavenly skies,
Or deep into the mysterious waters.
Living in a castle as a princess,
Again to wake up as a wandering lass,
Running aimlessly in the deep woods,
Suddenly collecting stones of diamond.

Thousands of emotions felt,
Surrealistic experiences,
Sometimes joy, sometimes grief,
The ultimate expedition of endless dreams.
All of a sudden,
My eyes opened wide awake,
A smile of relief,
Only to realise.

How beautiful a dream could ever be!
A dream is just not a dream,
It's a mystical reality,
Of untold truths, unknown self.
Deep rooted within self,
Reflecting your heart's desire!

Solace in Solitude

In the moonlit nights,
Walking along the beachside.

Humming the song of the waves,
Cool breeze kissing the cheeks.

The dancing clouds,
In the ballet of the star-studded sky,

Listening the music of silence,
Solace I find in this Solitude.

The talk with nature,
Gives flashes of insight!

Solitude, a journey of self,
Self-companion of joy!